Ancestor Count
Four Corner Poems

Jennifer Lisa Vest, Ph.D.

Metatron's Press
2020

First paperback edition Feb 2020

Book Cover designed by Sam_Designs1

Some of the poems in this book were previously published in the book "Names" by Jennifer Lisa Vest, published by Indigenous Speak, 1997;"Somebody Forgot to Tell Somebody Something was published by African American Review. 41. 3 (Jan 2008); "Names." Was previously published in the Canadian Journal of Native Studies, 30. 1(Spring 2010); "When" and "The Blanket" were published in Turtle Island To Abya Yala .Mica Valdez, ed. Malinalli Press, 2011; "For My Neighbors" Tongues, Vol. 4 (2004)

"Purple People" was published online @ Intermix: All The News & Views of The Mixed-Race Experience. http://www.intermix.org.uk (2007); "Some Good Done" The Multiracial Activist: An Online Magazine (2007);"Mixed Heritage Epic." Mestizo Revelations. Los Angeles: The Undeniables, June, 2010; "Bones" and "Traditional" The People Who Stayed: Southeastern Indian Writing after the Removal. Janet McAdams and Kathryn Walkiewicz, eds. Norman: University of Oklahoma Press, 2009; some of these poems were published in audio form in the following CDs: Mixed Messages Compilation CD (2009); Wonder Woman (2007); Camping at A Distance: Indigenous Recountings (2006); Ancestor Count: Purple People Poems (2006); some of these poems were first published on my Youtube channel: http://www.youtube.com/user/mxdpoet

ISBN 978-1-5011-7321-9 (paperback)
ISBN 978-1-4767-4660-9 (ebook)

www.drjenniferlisavest.com
Jennifer Lisa Vest, Ph.D.
Jennifer Lisa Vest is available for readings and
Philo-poetic performances.

Table of Contents

Grandma

For Mattye Leola Vest

When I asked
Grandma said, "Tell stories"
And I don't know
What kind of stories
And should they be written?
Or Told?
Novels or poems?
My grandmother's
Or my own?

When I was young she used to tell stories

From books
And from memory
I don't remember them
I was too young
And didn't know myself then
I learned history from a book

But
When I asked her
The most important question
When I asked her
After she was gone
About my purpose
She came all the way back
To respond
She said,
"Tell stories"

Chicago

For Micheal Lee Davis

We weren't poor, no
Just hungry and proud
Malden Street in Old Town
Before it was hip

No, it was always hip
Says my mother
There were white people
And brown people there
Immigrants and Jazz

We were foreigners by default
Hull House our haven
We knew Spanish by accident

We felt distinguished
By our lack of roaches
Sure we had lice
But everybody did

Free breakfast free lunch
Free afterschool program
A bus and two 'L's each morning
Sometimes we just swung
On the swings before school waiting

They called our mother once
Told her she couldn't do that
-But she worked so hard so far away
Two trains and all day-
Leave us there like that
Playground at dawn

One morning we found out why
Boys chased us into alleys
We threw up our
Carnation Instant Breakfast

Mommy always dressed us
Up real nice
Taught us to be polite
Kissed and hugged us tight

We never wore store-bought
Clothes they were all from scratch
Everything matched
If we were poor nobody told us

We were loved

Counting Ancestors

You ask me how much
How far back
What percentage
And I refuse

I refuse to count my ancestors for you

I won't do the math
Won't label the fractions
That make me whole
In your mind

I really don't mind
If you don't get it right
If you can't figure out exactly
What I am
Who I belong to
How to treat me
What my people are like

You see
My ancestors have
Become family
Across oceans of water
Across endless acres of land
Across many generations
And they have names
Which must be remembered
But not numbers

So
I will not count
My ancestors for you

Bones

They called us
The scientists called us
They said
Come get these bones

It's the law now
They passed a law now
They have to return
All those Indian bones

Into a cold cellar
They led us
To a box among many boxes
Many Boxes of bones

He was busy
The archeologist
He had work to do
Here it is he said
Handed us a box of bones
Here is it he said
Take it and go

We wanted to sing a song
But that room that man
It was so cold
We needed to sing a song
To burn some sage
We looked to the mountain
We looked for where to go

Without a ceremony
The right story
Some cedar some sweetgrass
We couldn't take
Those bones home

But even after we sang
Our songs we knew
Part of the story
Would always remain untold
Because we couldn't ask them
Somebody should have asked them
The part of the story
No one told

What were they thinking?
What were those people thinking
When they dug up
Our ancestors' bones?

When

Everybody wants to be an Indian
A pow-wow fancy-dancing
Feather-wearing Indian
Everybody wants to be the
Noble Savage of America
The old man on the banks of the river
Crying about pollution.

But who wants to live on the reservation
Bad coffee, beans, lard, diabetes
And too much TV
Who wants to farm on swampland
Bedrock and waterless sand?
Who wants to wrestle alligators for a living?

Everybody wants to wear suede
And fringe leather jackets
Patterns from Guatemala
Pretty beaded hair barrettes
And turquoise

But who wants to dress up
In fake Indian clothes
For snotty-nosed camp kids
Who call you "Hey Indian"
While you give them a tour
Of your culture?

Everybody wants to be an Indian
To be indignant about
"The crimes of white America"
To be spokesperson for the slighted
And the slaughtered
To write books about ecology
To teach workshops on herbology

But who wants to send their kids
To foreign schools that teach foreign language
Foreign culture
Shame
And how to disrespect?
Who wants to be laughed at in traditional dress
And told they have no culture
In the same breath?
Who wants to be idolized, romanticized
And iconized into something
You can never represent?

Everybody wants to be an Indian
A vision-seeking, sage-burning
Dream-catching Indian
Everybody wants to eat peyote
Dance at the Sundance
Sweat in the sweat lodge
Return to "the way things were"
And dress up like Pocahontas for Halloween

But who wants to have
 Sports teams
And four-wheel drives
Named after your ancestors
Or your tribe?
Who wants to be studied
And who wants to be questioned
And who wants their every action
Scrutinized
By non-Indians who claim
To know more than you do
About your way of life?

Everybody wants to be an Indian
When its popular
When its glamorous
When it's easy
When it's fun.

Colored

For Robert E. Vest, Jr

Uncle tells me
Grandfather always had
New Cadillacs, traded them in
Every two years
I remember he
Always dressed nice
Gave us bottomless bags of candy
How he used to tell me
No matter what
Grandpa loves you
His never-ending laugh

Years after his death Auntie
Tells me his first wife died
He was broken hearted
Before me met Grandma
He worked as a Bellhop
As a Janitor before I knew
Him as man who owned
A candy store and laughed

Uncle tells me that was
A good job for a Colored man
In those days
What was there to do
Back then
But shine shoes clean
Up for white folks
Pick somebody else's cotton?

Grandpa worked hard all his life
Grandpa's grandfather
Survived the Indian Wars
Grandpa's grandmother was a slave

Grandpa looked white
To me as I child
I asked how did Grandpa

Come to be Colored?
I learned early to ask who
Was what cause
Faces couldn't say
You had to hear the stories.

Colored wasn't a color
I found out
It was what you been through
And what the world done to you
What you made of yourself
Despite racism
It was how you survived

Grandpa saved his money
Grandpa married again
A beautiful brown lady
Who gave Grandpa
A dark brown skinned baby boy
He held tight all his life
Proclaiming to the world
Look at my child my perfect child
He looks just like me

Grandpa never said Black
Black and brown and red and
Yellow was all Colored
In our family you was Colored
And what shade you were
Didn't matter
What mattered was remembering
Where we came from
What mattered was loving one another

I remember him sitting
In his big green chair
A thin man
Perfectly dressed
With his leather slippers on
His hair combed to the side
Calling us kids to come running
When someone Colored
Came on TV
So we could be proud.

Maybe You're Not...

Maybe you're not a woman so
You don't know
Maybe you're not an Indian so
You don't care
Your house is comfortable
You go on vacation to "get away"

Maybe you're busy and you
Haven't noticed
Your mother is dying
Your children are confused
And you're a long long way from home

Maybe you're not Black so
You've never been
Arrested for no reason
Maybe you're not a woman so
You've never been raped
And been told it was your fault
Maybe you're not poor so
You've never lost everything

Maybe you're not paying attention
So you don't see the mountains crumbling
Maybe you're not listening
So you don't hear the trees crying
Maybe you buy bottled water
So you can't taste the difference

Uncle Frank

He tells me
He learned to stay alive by dreaming
By dreaming myself into existence
He says

Uncle Frank tells me he adopted
His identity because nobody would adopt him
Seven foster homes in five years
Three social workers
Two therapists
Nobody who understood

He tells me his Indianness
Was all he could remember
All he could claim
To maintain himself

He tells me he
Claimed new tribes
Every year
Chose new uncles
In every neighborhood
Told me
The foster parents never understood
His need to hang out downtown with the "drunks"
Drunk not the point, they were Indians
Staying alive
Somehow
Like him.

The Picnic

We tell it as a funny story
Brag about how we got a free ride
All the way down the mountain
We count ourselves lucky, say
Our ancestors sent that cop
Cause it was late and we were tired
And wanted to go home

We laugh about how that man
Just needed a picnic
Or a lover or maybe we shoulda
Just made him a sandwich
And sent him on his way

But on the side of the road
At sunset when he stopped us
Taking an afternoon hike
When his first question was
Did we speak English
It wasn't funny

Maybe it was the way
I wore the blanket
Across my shoulders
Looking like somebody's Indio
On the wrong side of the border

Our raggedy bag of potato salad and turkey sandwiches
My friend's GQ clothes
Maybe it was our complexions
Hers the color of roasted almonds
Mine of burnt copper

Something

Made us look like criminals
Made that cop want to arrest us
Almost arrest us!

Until I pulled out everything
Cited my student status
Used my most eloquent English
Asked that man with big innocent eyes
Do we look dangerous to you?
In the end he let us go
Even drove us halfway home
But that cop and me and my friend
We know

It wasn't because of our innocence
That things turned out that way
No, he let us go because of what he saw
In our eyes:

What he feared more than
Wetbacks in the wrong place
Vagrants, thieves or
Brownskins claiming to have rights

He let us go because he feared:
The danger we would become

Papa, Daddy, Dad, Man

For Robert E. Vest, III

Daddy
Polished handsome man
Running fast holding my hand
Til my feet take flight
In the tall grass
Because I could never keep up
Squealing squealing
I used to wonder
Would I ever keep up?

Daddy
No nonsense get good grades man
Come to school
Sit in the back of the class dad
Told the teacher don't ever hit my kid
Always a starched shirt, suit, and tie
"So distinguished, " said my friends

Daddy
Weekend single doing his best dad
Taking us to Foss Park
So we three
Could scream down that slide
One hundred times

Made us grilled cheese
Fought for us in court
Saved us from starving
In A foreign land
Wonder Dad

Learned spiritual man
Bought me endless books
Taught me "thoughts are things"
"You are what you believe"

Played me the recording of
Martin Luther King's
"I have a dream" speech

My father: Just you and me
Weekend excursions at dawn dad
Scrap wood at the lumberyard
Rock shows and pow wows
Religious Science tag team
Talking about life's meaning

Emotional crying hugging dad
Always kissed his Father
And his children on the lips
Loves us unabashedly man
Papa: Always know how much he misses me
A walking testament
There's an alternative
To toxic masculinity

The man who gave up his dreams for me
The man I have always tried to be
The only reason I got a PhD
The person who is always proud of me
A standard that has always guided me

Dad
You set the bar for my life
You are the sprinter who taught me how to fly
You let me know there is no ceiling only sky
And there are no words no words
With which to thank
Nothing I could do
No way I could ever pay
You back
For this life, man

Traditional

*For Don LittleCloud, Bonita Sizemore, Millie Ketchashawno, Bojack, and
Zenobia of the Black Native American Association in Oakland*

They told her
Her clothing
Was not traditional enough
for Grand Entry
they whispered
looked at her sideways
Asked her
what kind of Indian
Was she anyway?
And was she on the rolls?

They told her her hair
was too curly
and not traditional enough
for Grand Entry
Her skin too dark
suitable only for intertribal
Indians don't have blue eyes, they said
Indians don't have black skin, they said

And she could dance
You should have seen her!
And she could talk story!
You should have heard her!
And she knew medicine
You should have felt her!

But she wasn't traditional enough
for those urban Indians

So when those powwow Indians looked at me sideways
and started asking too many questions
She said come here little girl
Take this shawl, come and dance
And she taught me
how to be traditional.

[If not] For My Mother

For Michelle Lee Davis

If it weren't for my mother
Where and what would I be
Who would have taught me
How to stand strong fight back
How to think freely.

What kind of wimp would I be
Without her example
Without her ferocious story
She walked across a country
For my sisters and me

What kind of citizen
What kind of activist would I be
If she hadn't taught me
To challenge everyone
To question everything?

I wouldn't be
Painting paintings
Writing poetry/ would not love science
Wouldn't have all these degrees
Wouldn't eat organic
Recycle
Drive an old (gas-saving) car
Rock thrift sore fashion
Wouldn't recognize animals
As people
Trees as family
Wouldn't notice beauty
In everything

If not for my mother
It scares me to think
How I might have turned out
Who I would have become
If not for my mother.

When I Was Born

When I was born
King was planning his march on Selma
Kennedy was inaugurating
The NASA space program
And my parents were catching hell
From realtors who didn't want
To sell a house
To an interracial couple

My father says he was doing
His part to change things
By bringing a series of
Little mixed babies
Into the world

But my mother was
Afraid of the lives
We would be forced
To live

Because of desegregation
Affirmative action
My light skin
My [mother's] long hair
And King's people marching
I got educated I got a chance
I am a success story

People who don't know me
Find me beautiful
People who do know me
Don't understand

When I was born King said
"Things still aren't right in Selma"
And look- 35 years later-
They still aren't right

But I shouldn't complain
Because my mother was wrong
Or was she right?

About the life I would
Be forced to live.

You Look Like My People

You look like my people I tell her
Tracing the lines of my grandmothers
In the wrinkles around her eyes
The shape of her cheeks
Escaping from the center of her face
Like large brown mesas
Enchant me with memories

I try to explain simply say
Maybe we are distant kin
Where do you come from?
You look like my people

She laughs doesn't answer
Asks
Who are your people?

That's a long and confusing story I say and continue

With my questions
About this link
Until she too becomes
Mesmerized by my conviction
That there's a connection

We begin the investigation
Like a dance
With gentle probes
And speculations about blood
Geography, language, tradition

We take out paper, pens
Maps and photographs

Frantic for explanations
Search the shelves for snapshots
For the cousin, auntie
Ancestor who proves it
We sit close to touching
I trace my finger across her jaw
Try to grasp this resemblance
So familiar So elusive So real
But all these images and even imagination
Fails us

In our frustration
We resort to words write poetry
Remember weddings
Recite genealogies Retell family stories
We even make lists of Clans, race, tribes
Of people's names
Of place

In the end
Nothing exactly connects
We have it seems, few traditions in common
No kin to call cousins
But I don't believe
I refuse to accept
These unwelcome answers
These concrete but false conclusions

I claim her anyway

Names

We call ourselves
the Seminole people
Mikasuki, Creek, Oklawaha, Trail
But we've gone by other names
we won't translate
Names we can't repeat
that are nobody's business but our own
and other names
they didn't want us to keep

We come from many places
but we were always here

Before the Spanish came
We were Ikaniuksalgi
The **original** *Penisulares*
Kooti Bread eaters
Calusa, Timucua, Ais
Tekesta, Apalachee, Alacua
We were sailors, farmers, fishers
Our queens protected us
Our priests danced for us
Augustine was not our saint

They called us
fierce and powerful peoples
death-obsessed
serpent worshippers
giants and *smooth-faced pirates*
Before half of us left
for Cuba, Bahamas, Nicaragua
And the rest of us who survived
Spanish Christian kindness
baptism at the point of a sword
Escaped up North

Before the French came
We were Natchez, Biloxi
Alibami. Chitchimacha, Toltec
We venerated the women, the dead and the sun

With song, smoke, and shell-laden pyramids
We spoke many languages
We knew all our neighbors
They called us *moundbuilders*
sunworshipers
formidable foes

When they grew envious and impatient
before the messengers could gather
five nations of warriors
they killed women and children
fought a war of extinction
Those of us who weren't sold to English plantations
down south or to Haiti
Escaped to the East

Before the English came
we were Hitchiti, Cherokee
Yuchi, Yamassee
Tunica, Oconee
Many peoples coming together
Creating and recreating ourselves
Moving when necessary
united against a common foe
We became a nation of nations
We survived in our stories
We learned to love strangers
We traveled South
◇ ◇ ◇ ◇

Before Jackson
Before rabid flesh-hunting Carolinians came
We were fluid and raceless
Ibo, Dahomey, Ga Fon, Hausa, Yoruba
We were Ewe and Dogon
farmers teaching hunters
clans expanding
We were Mikasukee, Tallahassee, Muskogee
allies and kinfolk
Before they called us
Mulatto, Mestizo
Mustee, Negro
Stolen property
Creek

Before they tried to separate us out

One from another
We were families
Our neighbors called us
Eufala, Estee Seminolee
(Those who camp at a distance)
Remnants and renegades
Trailblazers and healers
Clever and careful
We fought war upon war
We called ourselves
Ki Tishshay, Looche, Hatke
Red, Black, and White
Esta Caddee
Esta Luske
Kanyuksa Esta Chattee
(People of the pointed land)
Regardless of oklee
We were Yatee
Human
We traveled in circles

But they could not defeat us
so they called us *savages*
Could not baptize us
so they called us *heathens*
Could not find us
so they called us *wiped out*
Could not understand us
so they called us *mysterious*
Could not educates us
so they called us *backwards*
Could not convince us
to learn their language
so they called us
hostile, shy, afraid

But they were like
Pahaykoshlay to us
And we Ayekchay
We had medicine for that

We kept moving
We took in strangers
We moved South
Back to the point
To a place where soft pink people

could not survive/many of their soldiers died
They took to passing laws
and telling stories about us

and they made up names

When they couldn't identify
Our diversity anymore
They called us
Florida Indians or
Florida Creeks or else
Seminoles
(convinced it was an English corruption
of *Cimarron*- Spanish for wildman)
And not the name our cousins gave us

When they got tired of fighting us
we became a legend
They spent a hundred years
Trying to find the
Last Unconquered Indians
Sent in the army
Government surveyors
Sports fisherman
Anthropologists
Missionaries
But we were untrackable
And intractable
When found

We cost the government
an embarrassment of riches
and dead white men

In their eyes
We were the *last frontier*
So they did what a man does
Who cannot fish
They drained the whole pond
In search of us

Brought in heavy machinery
And sucked dry
The glorious Everglades
Turned the swamps to
sand and rock and clay

rounded us up
To ask our names
        ◊ ◊ ◊

Some names are for lovers
Others are for friends
Our names are for our people
And we never told them to white men
We said: Sally, Tommy, Cypress, James
You didn't understand why we all had
The same names.

But before namegiving or namecalling
We were here
        ◊ ◊ ◊
We say
Before you left Spain in Search
of your splintered self
We were here
Before you realized England
Was cramped and dirty
We were here
Before you left France
For your piece of the pie
We were here
Before you tried to
Carve a nation
out of our expatriation
Before you defined your red-blooded
American selves
In terms of our absence
We were here
        ◊ ◊ ◊
Some names sort
Others deceive
These names tell stories
Historians
Refuse to believe

We call ourselves the Seminole people
Mikasuki, Creek, Oklawaha, Trail

We call you Ochkochay
The smoke in our eyes

Reckoning

There has been no reckoning
And until there is
What can we call ourselves
How can we claim ourselves
A country proud and unified
Possessing history?

We refuse to talk about it
We built our industry from it
We came to world power because of it
We killed 60 million in the name of it
We spent the last one hundred thirty seven years
Forgetting it
But we won't admit it

There has been no recounting
No remembering
No museums built
No monuments chiseled
No bold apologies
No heartfelt regret

There has been no reckoning
And until there is
What heritage can we claim ?
What destiny proclaim
When we are
Afraid of our past?

In This, The Fifth World

In this, the fifth world
Sweet green moss
Has a way of climbing
Out of rusty pipes
Into concrete cracks
Breaking and braiding through bricks
Weeds insist in coming up
Instead of other crops
In spite of gardener's chemicals
Ornate and specific stone paths

And trees

They have a tendency
To climb over fences
Airlift asphalt
Obstruct traffic lights
Drop leaves in the wrong place

But you and me
Are much more orderly

We believe in the bone of brick
The stature of steel
The insolence of iron gates

We've fallen victim to fences
Lines on the highway
The density of plaster

We think the boundaries are real.

Runaway Culture

I come from a long line of
Runaways escapees
Survivors outlaws
Border crossers and flagrant
Transgressors

So you see how silly
It sounds
You asking me to behave
As if I could when
It's not in my blood
And anyway
I wasn't raised that way.

Haiti

For Estes

Dreaming of Haiti
Lush green, people singing
Children running in the streets

I try to fly away at night
To this ancestral land
Where the people's eyes shine

America will have me
But Haiti knows me

From the marrow
Loves me from the soul
And Haiti waits for me I know

Say You're Sorry, Chapter 1

Some people want affirmative action
Some people want EOP programs
Some people want reparations
Some people want to get rid of these races
Some people just want to take a damn vacation
From these United States

What I want is simple
Requires no bureaucracy, no town hall
No administration
What I want does not need to be debated
Organized analyzed or allocated
I just want you to say you're sorry
In the end it all boils down to that

Say you're sorry
Say it like you mean it
Say it like you want to
Say it like you need to
Say it with a full heart
Say it like you can't stop
Over and over again

Say it till you lose your voice
Say it like you have no choice
I don't care if you're rich
I don't care if you're poor
I don't care if you're a radical
I don't care if you're married to one of us
Just say you're sorry
Say it like you mean it
Say it like you need to
Because you really need to
Its time you realized your need to
Say you're sorry

White people want us to forget it
Put it behind us
Nevermind it
It happened a long time ago they say
It's not relevant anymore they say
Stop talking about it they say

White people think amnesia is the answer
Black people think we should honor our ancestors
I think you should say you're sorry.

It's as simple as that.
Say you're sorry
Say you're sorry
Say it with a full heart
Say t from the back of your throat
Say it with a tear in your eye.
Say it like you want to save a life.
Just say you're sorry.
It's the least you could do
Just say you're sorry
Don't you think it's something you should do?

It's not much to ask for after 400 years
It's not much to ask for after all the terror
It's not much to ask for after all the money you made off
The sweat of our backs

Just say you're sorry
Say it like you mean it
Say it like you need to
Organize were sorry support groups
if you have to
Create the study of Sorry studies
if you have to
Hire tutors to teach other white people how to be sorry
if you have to
Learn mediation techniques so you can
get in touch with your inner sorry selves
If you have to

Just say you're sorry
Say it from way deep inside your soul
Don't make excuses
Just say you're sorry.

Don't tell me why you don't have to
Don't tell me why you don't want to
Don't tell me why it won't matter if you say it
It matters
Trust me on that
Say you're sorry
See what happens
If nothing happens say it again
If nothing happens say it louder
If nothing happens get a megaphone and shout it from the rooftops...

Just say you're sorry

For the Racist ...

I almost tell her I love her
Whisper it into her ear
Would the shock kill her?

She doesn't know me
But knows somehow
That she hates me
Deep in her bones
Recoils from me
The image of me
The symbol I seem

She does not know me

What if I took that leap
Leaned over told this stranger
I do not know

This stranger
So full of guile
What if

Across this shiny counter
In this public place
I told her that I loved her

Would the shock kill her
Or would she be transformed?

Some Wounds

There are some wounds that never heal
No amount of tending pretending
Careful concentrated concern
Nor Positive neglect release of regret
Some sores nothing erases nothing cures

Bandages don't hide scars refuse to fade
Some wounds are for life
Testimony to strife tell on us
Broadcast to the world
Accusations in the flesh
Let everybody know what got left
What was undone what mourning
Song was sung what can't be forgot
What and who after all we have become

There are some wounds
Red gashes of pain
Raised black and brown
Welts remain some scars
That grow larger not smaller
With time.

Some wounds that mark us
Stain the soul, set one forever apart
Cause people to stare and start
Some wounds that can't be glanced at
Never become commonplace, happenstance
Never get replaced by glory funny stories
The champion's parade
Never become red badges of courage.

And these are the wounds
Nobody talks about

Everybody sees
These are the wounds nobody wants
Everybody runs from nobody seeks
Everybody shuns

Which is why
These are the wounds that never heal
We refuse to believe they're even real
It seems easier somehow
Never mind the screaming bleeding tirades
In the end we just refuse
To be marked
By something we can't change rearrange
Overcome unravel or defeat

Still
There are some wounds that never heal
Wounds that are for life
Testimony to strife
Evidence in the flesh
Let everybody know what succumbed/what died
What did and didn't survive
What and who after all we have become

Turning Tortillas

You were making tortillas
I felt the need to be near you
Talking watching hovering around
Lots of mujeres in the kitchen

I'm watching your hands:
Pick up first one flip turn
Put one down

I pretend to help get scolded
For burning the bread
My hands fumble my eyes glide
She can't even turn tortillas!
You tease
Everybody laughs
My tortillas are black

I laugh the hardest
The truth makes me
Blush with blue smoke in my hair

My Tia taught me well
How to make tortillas
When I was young
But I didn't come into the kitchen
For that

Yes, We Did

For my students

When I got the job offer
People told me not to take it
Said The South
Is too racist sexist homophobic
For someone like me

They might have been right
But I came here anyway
Told them it may be that way now
But I'm gonna change it

I will teach those racists
How to love Black and Brown people
I said
I will teach those sexists how to love women and girls
I said
I will teach those homophobes
How to love The Queers

And I will gather up
The Young Ones
Teach them to rebel
Against the hatred of their elders
And together all the young ones
They will change things
Yes they will

Its been 7 years
And I changed things
Yes, I did.
Maybe not enough
To save my own skin
But we changed things
Yes we did
My students and I made a difference
We changed things, yes we did.

Dangerous Liasons

I almost don't let myself
Touch you feel you know you
As if I know this is a door
I can't back out of

Some rooms have two exits
Your room has none
Everywhere I walk carefully laid lasers
Anticipate my misstep

I am only two kisses away from
Tripping an alarm
That will reveal me
If I am too eager or too bold
I will get caught
We both know this

But something inside me
Has become a large heavy ball
Careening downhill towards the intersection
I can see the danger
But seductive energy is a law unto itself

Even the most desperate
The most determined person
Cannot stop
A renegade train
From jumping the tracks

I almost don't call you
Don't ask you don't touch you
Don't taste you don't take you
But I do

All my butts, whatifs
All my concerns and quandaries
All my hesitation and regret
Simply become foreplay

I am afraid but...
I am also persuaded
All the questions I have
Get quelled by kisses

I almost don't but I do
Wondering what's wrong
Gets outweighed
By my wanting you

My resistance is not resolve
But merely a core of cold hard metal
Slowly liquefied
By the hot white
Persistence of your desire

Tribute

For JilChristina Vest

If she knew
She wouldn't let lovers dis her
Would never settle
Would tear down everyone else's hesitation
With her own sure self
Would see herself in mirrors
Strut around bigger and badder than life
Wouldn't admire other folks so much
Would find her own voice
Amplify it on somebody's loudspeaker
Wake us all up/send us
Crashing into the streets
Talkin' bout
We gotta find her
Gotta follow her
Gotta hear what she want

If she knew
She wouldn't be nobody's fool
Wouldn't believe anybody
Tell her she not supersmart
Wouldn't let
No racist professors
No doggish men
No family members or friends
Suggest she was
Anything less than perfect

And then
She'd break out of hiding
All those lyrical lines
Filed away in fabric-covered journals
-she'd read her poetry in public-
Force us all to listen
To the screaming
Tender tirade of her watchfulness
The wonder of her words
Subject us to the verses
She's been composing
In closets all these years.

Michigan Summers

Is it true
That I can never go back
Ride on Grandpa's
Lawnmower tractor
On Grandpas shoulder
In Goguaq lake
Jump off the high dive
Catch baby frogs
Make go-carts
Swim at the Y
And
Sneak oreos out of
Grandma's cookie jar
In a Michigan summer?

Is it true
They sold the house
And Teddy, our blue bunny?
And grandpa's bar
With the poker chips
The patio they built
The swingset
The path between the
Hedges looking out
Over the hill
Where the forbidden kids played
Grandma's fried chicken
Father johns
Every morning
Those decade-long piles
Of Jet and Ebony magazines?

Is it true
Grandpa's dead
And grandma can't talk
And were all grown up
Forgetting about Michigan
Forgetting about
Our Michigan summers?

Fridays

On Mondays
My people are brown
Burnt sienna colored
Big sky-touching hair
More despised in everybody's eyes
Than any other race
We believe in the spirit
Live it /dream it/ dance it
Fight to survive

On Tuesdays
My people are red
Copper-colored with slick thick hair
More romanticized in everybody's eyes
Than any other race
But still denied a place
Surrounded by skeletons and broken bottles
We fight to live/ in the present

On Wednesdays
I refuse a race
Check too many boxes
Talk in contradictions
Change my mind by the minute
Talk in riddles

On Thursdays I have conversations
About the politics of peopleness
I strategize, theorize, criticize
And come to a culturally specific conclusion
About who I should be
All things considered

Then there's Fridays...

Somebody Forgot to Tell Somebody Something*

*(Written in response to the referendum passed by the
Seminole Nation of Oklahoma to disenfranchise tribal members of
African descent)*

Something happened at Seminole
Something stunning, something sad
Somebody forgot
In the seventh month
Of the 16th decade after
Their unwilling surrender
Somebody among the
Survivors of three wars
Somebody, after encountering
Three types of treacherous whites
Somebody, after three forms of federal foulplay:
After being Allotted, Terminated and Reorganized

Somebody forgot
Somebody forgot

And these striking stricken people
Started to divide themselves up.
How is it? How is it?
How could it? Who would've?
Somebody forgot to tell somebody something
How else to explain
A people dividing itself up
After the conquest.
How else to explain a people saying
Ancestors don't, history don't, kinship don't matter
Only race?
Somebody, maybe somebody's mother
Somebody, maybe somebody's son
Somebody forgot to sing the songs
Somebody forgot to tell the stories
No honor stories, no honor stories for the dead.
How else to explain?
Three hundred years of struggle evaporated
In a single election?

How else to explain
People claiming Seminole and fullblood
in the same breath?

How else to explain
Disowning relatives for the white man's money, guns,
And high stakes bingo games?
How else to explain?

Somebody forgot to remember

Who we are
Who we were
Who we have been and how we got here.
Somebody forgot to remember:

The Yamassee Seminole "slaves" married in.
Somebody forgot to remember":'
The numerous and fumbling fragments of bands
Finding each other in Florida,
Escaping, cascading into new places, new races
Calling each other kin.

Somebody forgot to remember
We weren't always the Seminole tribe
Just one more band of ragged
Survivors escaping the spreading plague
Of Europeans marching across the land.

Somebody forgot what the word Seminole stands for;'
What it means

Somehow, with all the stories our grandmothers told us
Somehow, with all the pride we carry about puffed up
in our patch- work shirts
Somehow, after five reservations, two languages, and three countries
Somebody forgot to tell somebody something
And we have forgotten who we are.

How else to explain
The separation General Jessup set in motion
Being finished up by modern so-called Oklahoma Seminole?

How else to explain
Reviving the legacy of Indian Commissioner Harris
Skilled separator of Indians by color
Renowned returner of suspiciously dark-skinned
Cherokee, Seminole and Creek
To the white planters who claimed them as slaves?

Somebody forgot to tell somebody something

Somebody forgot the ancestors too
Somebody forgot the hundreds of
"Black Indians" who died at the fort, the Negro Fort
In Apalachicola
So that the "red" Indians might live;

And somebody forgot all the red-skinned men and women
Who died in the first Seminole war
Rather than separate out the "so-called blacks" from within.

Somebody forgot to remember
the demands of Chief Alligator and Micanopy
Who said they wouldn't move West without the guarantee
That the dark-skinned black and half-breeds among them
Would be allowed to come with.

And somebody forgot
The ancestors who died at Mulatto Girls Town,
Who died at Payne's Town, at King Heijah's Town,
At Bucker Woman's Town;
all so-called Seminole Negro Towns.

Somebody forgot Mulatto King of Cho-co-nickla Town, too.

Nobody did but somebody shoulda
Told those Indians
Holed up at Wowoka in Oklahoma
About the half-breed Seminole John Horse
Who founded that town,
Who fought with Osceola and Wildcat
Who traveled to Washington
Who for being Black was forced to flee to Mexico
In search of an elusive justice he never received.

But somebody forgot to tell somebody something
It seems so many stories have been forgot
The ashes of our ancestors blow about unrecognized
And we have forgotten where we came from
Who we once were
And how we have come to exist.
How else to explain
A people dividing itself up After the conquest?

*Title borrowed from a piece by Barbara Christian who borrowed it
from Toni Morrison.

Camping at a Distance

I call myself Seminole
And know refutations abound
I have been camping at a distance my whole life
Whose kinfolk am I?

I make my own fire
Mimicking the fires nearby
I sew my own patchwork
Mimicking the grandmothers I have known
I cook my own lonely pot of sofkee
Who dare eat with me?

I call myself Seminole
And questions abound
My ties are tenuous
My self- naming suspicious

But I know who I am
Exiles tend to have the most vivid
The most tenacious memories
We tend to sing the songs the loudest
Though often off-key.

I call myself Seminole
I camp at distance
I have never left yet
Am forever traveling home

Perching

Black cracking
Comes again the pain

Then too this anger
The stark white cage

My fist my face
The glass and then

No matter I destroy
This space

Or weep
Or scream

My heart is magenta
Against this velvet night

And I am just

A soft brown girl
Perching on this life.

Some Will Say

If asked
Everybody will have a theory
A diagnosis for me
A cause for this effect
An explanation for this aberration
Everybody will claim to know the reason
I turned out this way

Some will say
I fell victim to their voices
To the softening lull
The overwhelming harmony
Of their humming calls
Or the tender touch of their skin
Stretching and trembling
Against the innocent tension
Of mine

Others will claim it was
A weakness in me
An open wound
Something wanting within
My simple suggestibility
Making me victim to their whims

Some will say I have suffered
From bad men, bad sex,
Bad mothering or bad advice
That I couldn't help myself
That I don't know myself
That I haven't been treated right
And I just need someone to treat me different
To treat me better, to turn me out

And they always have themselves in mind

There are some who will say

They bore witness to the witchery
Say they were there
Saw the sirens seduce me
Saw how powerless I was
An easy victim of left-handed magic
Of naked and bewitching desire
They will say they saw the Brujas
And hoodoo women
They will remember brickdust, high john
Stolen hair and names on red paper
They will say I was overpowered
Outsmarted, easily fooled
And they will want to rescue me

Others will be less sympathetic
And more vindictive
But they will be justified
In their disdain
Because, they say
I am perverse, oversexed
Insatiable somehow
Selfish, rebellious
A woman who expects an orgasm every time!
Kinky and shallow- an island
Cause if I don't want a man I must not want
Children, a family, community
It must be all about me- just a sex thing

Nobody will guess correctly
No one will suggest the obvious

So many will fail to see the love in this thing
Its simplicity
The joy the beauty the romance
The ecstasy
So few will see it clearly
But everybody will have a theory
A diagnosis for me
Everybody will claim to know the reason
I turned out this way

Mixed Heritage Epic

I am a person of mixed heritage
Africans may not claim me
Nor Native Americans
Nor Europeans either
But I am a person of mixed heritage
And I claim all my ancestors

Those who
Raised me
And those I only know if in dreams
Those who betrayed me
And Those who demy me
Those that I look like
Those that I don't
Those my parents talk about
Those my parents won't

I claim my relations
Like I claim my lives
Whether/regardless
They recognize me.
What they don't teach me
I learn in their books
What they will not tell me
I overhear and repeat
I wear their clothes and their customs as my own
And I come to their ceremonies
Without invitation.

I cook their food
And pass down their legends
I tell their stories and make them mine
I know their dances
Sing their songs
I pray to their gods
I know then
I have dissected them
So I understand why
They hate me.

For you see I am not simply a woman
A black a brown, a white, a red woman
But so much more and so much less
For in the eyes of many
The history of the half-breed is me
I am a symbol of several centuries
The fruit of
Lost seeds
Mistaken hybreed
I am the definition of the forbidden
I am the aftermath of rape
The constant daily visual reminder of
The savagery of conquest
The mother's torture
The disintegration of a people
The disappearance of a race

And I have been the deadly
Double agent
The imposter
The traitor
The broker
The mercenary
The savior
The sacrifice
The messenger
The thief

And I have done the unspeakable
To the underdog
My own mothers people
I have been the Judas
Have given the kiss that crushed a culture
Whispered the secrets
That disclosed the sacred
Led the marauders to the
Temples and

Hid myself in the leaves of the ancestor tree
And watched.

And I have been the scout and the interpreter
Translating the rage of my people into

A treaty of transgression
And I have been the one
Who told the
The master and the colonel
When they came
That I could lead my people to the table
To discuss their own defeat.

I have been the foundation of self hatred
Have set beauty standards and political agendas
And I have been the leadress of a movement to deny
I have Denied myself
Have denied my blackness
Have shunned my redness
Have hidden my golden lineage
I have lied to myself
I have lied and got ovah
I have lain with the enemy
And then

When that wasn't enough
I have become the enemy myself
And prided myself in it.

But I am more than my history
And more than the symbol I seem
I am a soft skinned human being
And I have also cried myself to sleep
Many a night.

For you see I was always the bastard
The unfortunate conception
The evidence of sin
The trick baby
I was called imposter
Outsider
Child a of a whore
Half-breed
Mutt
Zebra
paleface
Mulatto
Two-tone
redbone
slut

I was shunned
And I was denied
I was accused of crimes I was not alive
To commit
And
I am asked to explain the actions of people
Who are not my kin
And I am blamed for massacres
And genocide
And the prostitution of a race
And I am asked to bow my head in shame
For what my parents did
And what my existence represents.

And I am too red to be black
Too black to be red,
Too brown to be white.

And I have been I have been discussed
And discounted, denounced and
Discarded and put into a tragic box.

I have been paraded around like a clown
And I have been
Betrayed in the worst way
And told I was an accident in the flesh.

And when after being pushed aside
By everybody's size and texture and shade requirements
I cried out in self discovery,
In mixedblood pride
I was laughed at or ignored
Told I was the child of a war
And had no right to celebrate my birth.

And I was told instead
I had to chose
A real race
A real people
A real identity
Not really my own

And I was told I could be either or
One or the other
Black white red
One and one only

One per person
Ad that
I must be confused
And if necessary one cold be chosen for me
And no I couldn't choose to be black on Mondays an Indian on
Tuesdays
And mostly I just need to make up my mind
Cause what about the revolution?

And nobody wants to hear any more
Stories about the tragic mulatto

But I am a woman of mixed heritage.
Black red white brown other colored
My color
And I claim all my relations
I am African Indian European and none of the above
I am a child of my mother's womb.

I am the other
The other's other
Not the other problem
I am mixed lineage
Mixed blood mixed culture
Not mixed up

I am the exception
Exceptional
The new box the axe holder
And the box breaker
And I am the ally my people's need
The messenger they seek
The translator they crave
The future they fear
The bridge builder they desire

And I am the question you must answer

Can't Help Remembering

He says his family never got over it
He says they hung his uncle
Without warning
The day before the wedding
To his intended
A white man's daughter

Get him, hold him
The sound of the crowd pushing in
The scratching gravel
Drag of his feet
The menacing smiles
The frayed rope held
In the callused hands
Of red-faced choking men

He says our family
Can't help remembering
He says they spent their lives
Trying to forget.

Niko

So little but so strong
You throw your brother into
The air and laugh

You are silent
When others are crying
You are a rock
A tiny tiny shiny rock

And I want to grab you
Shake you make you
Promise me not to be
So strong so strong
Chocolate cherub child
Giggly gorgeous girl

You don't have to know
Everything womanchild
Sometimes you can be wrong

Don't grow up to take care
Don't hide your feelings
Share
Don't make yourself small
For anyone
Don't be the rock
Others rely upon

You don't have to be strong
And you don't have to float and fly and flit
Away, you can stay
Present be here
Be fully YOU in every way

Malik

I wrote this poem for you
Because once I saw you crying
Because I never could bare it
Your loss
Your loneliness your
Being sick or sad or sorry

I don't know if this poem can heal you
But I will it to:
I let loose these words
Like hot hands
Hovering over your wounds
I cradle you with imagined arms
Singing away your tears

The sky is dimmer
When you do not shine
The sound of silence
Misses your happy laugh
Jiggle juggle joy
Little lovely boy
Come back come back
Climb into my lap

Promise me be happy
Rise up shine and shimmer
The world is waiting
The future holds its breath
Its you we need
On you we depend

The Blanket

When young, our passion
Is ripe like soft fruit
We are mischievous
Our love is abundant
Our eyes are greedy.

We welcome into our blankets
Whoever is tender and smiling
Whoever will yield
To our elastic
Touch and giggle

We wrap and cover
Whoever will take this moment
Like a hot corn cake
In cold hungry hands
Eating quickly and
Savoring nothing

When we grow older
We talk of time differently
We try to hold onto
Things untouchable
We try to name
What is un-namable

We sew buttons
Onto our blankets
Reach for wind
And cry when it evades us

We become nervous and cocky
We begin to think we know
What we want

We spend less time
In the blanket.

Prep School Days

For Julia Vest

We brown girls
Too much curl

They so rich
Skip school ditch

Prep school daze
We plot maze

They disdain
Broke kid pain

Mixed girls way:
Get good grades

They shop lift
Act as if

We lay low
They don't know

Dumb don't cost
They stay lost

We laugh long
We stay strong

They side eye
We sky high

Prep school daze
Mixed girl ace

Sister team
We succeed

Not Quite Right

For Jacob Braxton

He says there is something
She says there is something
Not quite right about me

You know what I mean
Something is not quite right
About you too!

Absence where there should be presence
Flat where there should be curves
Round where you should be narrow
Hairy where you should be smooth

Not quite right kid not quite right
Are you a chick or a dude?
Shave already lady, get a wax
Boy, Stop bein' so damn dramatic
Cut your hair already be a man

Something not quite right
About my talk my walk
The way I sit
the volume of my voice
The spread of my arms
The way I take up space

The arrogance of my confidence

You know what I mean
Something is not quite right About you...too

Gotta be.
Something just not right
About opting out
Refusing to choose
Failing to care about pronouns

Salt in the wound

Androgynous
Ambiguous
Fickle fab- ridiculous

Must be
There is something not quite right
Something too much
Too loud too strong
Too wrong

And something also not enough
Not sweet not soft not girl enough
Not tough not rough not boy enough

So
annoying
so
uncommitted
so TOTALLY unclear

Too much and not enough
You know what I mean
You have been too much too inbetween

Tiptoeing like you do
Left to right
Dim to bright

Breaking slow then
Accelerating recklessly into the curve

Streaking back and forth like we do
Across this painstaking heartbreaking boundary
A dangerous dance we choose

Like we don't know
Like nobody told us the rules
Like we haven't heard the threats

We thwart so many conventions
Wear fashion so recklessly fantastic
It could
Get us killed

But still we dance
Like our truth is stronger than their fists
Like ambiguity will last longer
Than these binaries these myths

Like we can refuse to pick one pick two
Like we could pick both be both
Or pick the wrong one
Be neither nor

One gender
two genders
Three genders
four

Like being Indians we could choose
Indigenous terms, Indigenous roles,
Two Spirit,
Nadli,
Ha-wa-me,
Na-pa-ya-ken

Like being Africans we could
Remember a time when
We honored
Sacred men who were gentle
Sacred Warrior Women

Like we should
Be celebrated for who we were born to be
Again

No
Must be something not quite right

About you
About me

Cause
We have too much nerve
Too many ovaries/cajones
for our
Own damn good

Parading our strangeness around like we do
Too much love for our own
Damn good
Too much faith in the way we are
Not the way we should

Be
Yeah.
Something not quite right
About you about me
About they about zee

Too much and not enough
Of everything we were supposed to be...

Sacred space
Tell them
We are holding sacred space
One gender two genders
Three genders four

Some Good Done

Biologically I am
A mixture more and less
Complicated than I claim to be
Culturally

My mother my father they
Have their own identities
My phenotype is another story
Entirely

Where I grew up and how
Who my ancestors were
And why they died
All conspire to define me
In ways that are beyond even me.

Ambiguity is my home
Either/or does not apply
And my existence defies
So many names and claims
Of place
It would be a lie to check a race

All I know for certain
Is that it matters
That my existence
Confounds you
That your inability to classify me
Bewilders you
And there is some good done
Each time I cause confusion
There is some good done

Demands of Existence

If I told you to do the impossible
To fight the impossible fight
To pursue the impossible dream
If I told you it was the only thing that would
Make you possible
Would you do it?

If I told you your life was absurd And unfair
And the cards stacked Ridiculously against you
But that you should live nonetheless
That you must live nonetheless
Would you do it?

If I set wolves at your door and put snakes in your bed
If I made your neighbors vultures
And your enemies your only friends
If I gave you but a stone for a pillow
And a shack for a home
And told you to awaken each morning
With a plan
To awake each morning
Determined to live
Would you do it?

If I gave you but one hawks feather to pray with
And 7 rocks set in a circle for a temple
If your flock was a ragged and desperate band of thugs
Your father a murderer and your own mother addicted to drugs
Would you have the strength to lead them?
Would you have the heart to love them?
Would you have the humility to call yourself one of them?
To claim their faults as your own?

If I colored you black and set you down in this white world
If I shaped you woman and set you down in this man's world
If I fashioned you queer
And set you down in this straight world
If I told you to do the impossible
To fight the impossible fight
To pursue the impossible dream
If I told you it was the only thing that would Make you possible
Would you do it?